WASTED!

FATBERGS, SPACE JUNK, PLASTIC

AND A LOAD OF OTHER RUBBISH

CLIVE GIFFORD

First published in Great Britain in 2020 by Wayland

Cover artwork: Andy Smith
Design: Lisa Peacock / Rocket Design (East Anglia) Ltd
Editor: Nicola Edwards

ISBN: 978 1 5263 1397 3 (HB)
ISBN: 978 15263 1398 0 (PB)

10 9 8 7 6 5 4 3 2 1

Wayland, an imprint of
Hachette Children's Group
Part of Hodder and Stoughton
Carmelite House
50 Victoria Embankment
London EC4Y 0DZ

An Hachette UK Company
www.hachette.co.uk
www.hachettechildrens.co.uk

Printed and bound in Dubai

Picture acknowledgements:

Alamy: Mary Andrews 25; imagegallery2 21c; Paolo Oliveira 27t, 46br.

Dreamstime: Alanesspe 15b; Lexandr Lexandrovich 14b; Lillian Tveit 27cr.

EPFL: 41c.

ESA: David Ducross.

Getty Images: Aminu Abubakar/AFP 29c; José Azel/Aurora Open 36b; Adrian Dennis 10bl, 11; KSC/NASA 40bl; James Leynse 23; Mirrorpix 8 inset; Yasser Al-Zayyat/AFP 47t.

Greenpeace: Fred Dott 31b; Justin Hoffman 30b; Wolf Wichmann 31t.

Robert Harding: Iqbal Kusumadireza 19.

NASA: JSC 38b, 39t.

Shutterstock: Mohamed Abdulraheem 16 inset; addkm 10brl; Muhammad Qadri Anwar 28t; Stephane Bidouze 17b; Blulz60 43t; Kanittha Boon 27bl; Pete Burana 33c; buteo 20c; Coffeemill 6b; Mike Flippo 3br; frantic00 29t; Kev Gregory 27c; GrooveZ: 21t; Indonesiapix 24b; Jirik V: 34; Stanislava Karagyozova 28b; kosmos111 18; A_Lesik 12t; LukeandKarla.Travel 9b; Roman Mikhailiuk 4-5p; ND700 10brc; Nemova Oksana 37ca; OvuOng 37cb; Papakah 26; petratrollgrafik 13c; Picsfive 3bl; Pixavril 45t; PongMoji 12c; Suradech Prapairat 3tr,43bl; Salvacampillo 24t; sergey0506 10br; Silent Corners 20b; Skycolors 15tr; thanis 7c, 46bc; anutr tosirikul 21b; Lee Yiu Tung 42b; Video Media Studio Europe 16; De Visu 17t; Vladi333, elements furnished by NASA 40tr; Pande Putu Hadi Wiguna 44b; zzphoto.ru 37b.

Thames Water: 10t, 12b.

The OceanCleanUp: 32b,33b.

Topfoto: 8.

Wikimedia Commons: Marlenenapoli CC1. 35t; Muntaka Chasant CC4. 35b;

US Airforce/PD: 41t.

Every effort has been made to clear copyright. Should there be any inadvertent omission, please apply to the publisher for rectification.

The website addresses (URLs) included in this book were valid at the time of going to press. However, it is possible that the contents or addresses may have changed since the publication of this book. No responsibility for any such changes can be accepted by either the author or the publisher.

CONTENTS

WHAT A WASTE! _____ 4

GREAT SMOGS _____ 6

FATBERGS! _____ 10

ISLANDS OF RUBBISH _____ 14

RUINED RIVERS _____ 18

GIANT LANDFILLS _____ 22

THE PROBLEMS WITH PLASTIC _____ 26

ALL AT SEA _____ 30

WHAT A DUMP! _____ 34

SPACE WASTE _____ 38

YOU v. WASTE _____ 42

GLOSSARY _____ 46

FURTHER INFORMATION _____ 47

INDEX _____ 48

WHAT A WASTE!

Human beings have always been a wasteful species. Archaeologists have discovered rubbish piles containing broken pottery, arrowheads and food waste, such as shellfish shells and animal bones, that are thousands of years old. Today, each of us generates many kilogrammes of waste each week, often without thinking about it.

RUBBISH GENERATORS

Waste levels have soared as the number of people on the planet has boomed. By 2024, the global human population will reach eight billion people – double the number there were in 1974. Not only are there many more people on the planet but, on average, each person is generating far more waste than in the past. In the United States, a typical household of five people now throws away 3,600 kg of rubbish every year – that's about the weight of 20 gorillas.

SHOCKING STATISTICS

Waste isn't just old newspapers, drinks cans and food packaging, it's also food itself. The United Nations estimates that a third of all food produced in the world for people is never eaten. This waste is equal to more than 3.5 million tonnes of food every single day of the year – enough to feed hundreds of millions of people.

Waste can cause serious pollution, damage habitats for people and other living things and consume huge amounts of other valuable resources to deal with it. Rubbish dumps occupy large areas of land that could be used for housing, farming or left unspoilt as homes for plants and wildlife. Transporting waste away from where it's created also uses vast amounts of energy.

This book takes a look at some of the worst results and biggest impacts of people's wasteful ways of life, the effects on the environment and local people and some of the ways these problems are being tackled. It ends with ideas for things we can do to reduce waste and help the planet.

GREAT SMOGS

Harmful waste substances, such as the gases sulphur dioxide and carbon monoxide, enter the air due to natural processes like erupting volcanoes, but also because of human activity. When air pollution is concentrated and trapped at ground or near-ground level in a busy town or city, it can cause a deadly haze called smog.

↓ Burning fossil fuels like coal and oil in motor vehicles or to generate heat or electricity produce large quantities of air pollution as do some processes in industry.

CAUSES OF SMOG

Smog gets its name from combining the words smoke and fog. In the past, particles from smoke caused by wood and coal fires would mix with water vapour in the air to form a thick, toxic fog.

Another type of smog is the haze caused by nitrogen oxides (particularly from motor vehicle emissions) and volatile organic compounds (VOCs) – chemicals released by industry and in some paints and cleaning products. These undergo complex chemical reactions with sunlight to produce harmful ground-level ozone and tiny solid specks of air pollution called particulates.

BREATHING BAD

Smog can make breathing more difficult, inflaming eyes, nose and your airways and lodging particulates in your lungs. It can severely affect and even kill vulnerable people such as the young, elderly and those with asthma, bronchitis, emphysema and heart or lung conditions.

↑ People wear face masks in smog-ridden Bangkok – Thailand's largest city. In 2019, more than 400 schools were forced to close, to protect children from harmful air pollution, and people were encouraged to stay indoors.

STATS OF SHAME

According to the World Health Organization (WHO), 4.2 million people die every year due to outdoor air pollution including smog.

THE GREAT SMOG OF LONDON

London had long suffered heavy air pollution which would form thick, suffocating fogs or smogs nicknamed 'pea-soupers'. In December 1952, heavy pollution, from homes and factories burning coal as well as from rising numbers of motor vehicles, became trapped close to the ground by weather conditions. The resulting Great Smog brought the city to a standstill for five days.

Most drivers couldn't see through the gloom, cars were abandoned and ambulances couldn't run. Accidents and crime increased and more than 4,000 people died, mostly from breathing problems or diseases.

Visibility was so poor during the Great Smog that police officers used flares to signal to drivers. Sometimes bus conductors even walked ahead of their vehicles to show drivers the way through the smog.

THE BIG CLEAN-UP

The Great Smog prompted new laws in Britain and the creation of 'smokeless zones' in the cities as well as increasing the use of smokeless fuels. Many cities around the world continue to suffer with smog and use a range of methods to tackle it. Key ways include providing more public transport, banning certain fuels or substances and reducing petrol-burning motor vehicles on city streets.

QUALITY TWEETS

In 2016, 10 pigeons wearing air monitoring sensors in little backpacks were released in London to measure the city's air quality. The sensors sent back regular measurements as *PigeonAir* Twitter tweets!

NO-DRIVE DAYS

Mexico City is located in a basin surrounded by hills which means that winds struggle to disperse air pollution. In the early 1990s, the city's air was some of the most heavily polluted in the world. The city authorities set up bike-sharing networks and increased public transport. *Hoy No Circula* or 'No-Drive Days', banned motorists for at least one day a week from driving around the city. While there has been some improvement in air quality, much work remains to be done.

FATBERGS!

↓ A fatberg clogs up a sewer pipe in London, UK.

In the past, waste was sent directly into rivers, stinking pools known as cesspits or left on the streets, often contaminating clean water and spreading disease. Sewer systems now carry away huge amounts of waste from buildings. They have improved public health greatly but some are under threat from giant waste blockages known as fatbergs.

IN A FOG

Fatbergs are made of two groups of things mixed together. Fats, oils, such as cooking oil, and grease (together known as FOGs) enter the sewer system where they mix with wet wipes, plastic nappies and other solid waste which people have thrown down toilets and drains. The two bind together to form giant, often solid, lumps.

↑ Fatbergs are hard to break down and they stink - sewer workers describe the stench as a mixture of rotting meat and a really foul-smelling toilet.

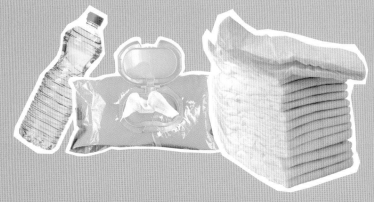

CLOGGING CITIES

Fatbergs have been found in many city sewers around the world. One caused damage to a sewage treatment plant in Eleebana, Australia, in 2016. Another the following year, in the Spanish city of València, cost over two million Euros to remove. Also in 2017, the 'Monster of Whitechapel' was discovered in a London sewer. Weighing over 120 tonnes, this fatberg isn't even the biggest found in the UK. That prize goes to a monster blockage found clogging up a sewer in Liverpool in 2019. Longer than three Boeing 747 jumbo jets, this gigantic fatberg weighed an estimated 400 tonnes – that's the weight of 65 African elephants!

↓ A sewer worker examines a portion of the giant Whitechapel fatberg. Parts of this mass were cut off, dried out and displayed at the Museum of London.

FLOODING

Large fatbergs can create major blockages of city sewer pipes. These blockages prevent waste water reaching sewage treatment centres where it would be cleaned and processed. Instead, the sewage backs up and may escape out of drains or flow back up and into household sinks and toilets. Urgh!

↓ When heavy rainfall occurs, blocked sewers can lead to widespread flooding of a city's streets. This creates the risk of a revolting and potentially disease-spreading mix of rainwater and raw (untreated) sewage (inset, right).

FAT-FIGHTERS

Utility companies in the UK spend over £100 million a year removing fatbergs from clogged pipes and tunnels. Most of the work is hard labour, with staff known as flushers (left) using pickaxes, shovels and, sometimes, high-pressure water pumps to break up the solid fatty masses. The material then has to be brought to the surface. Even with teams working shifts, a large fatberg can take many weeks to remove.

EAT IT UP!

A company in Germany called Lipobak is trialling using large numbers of fat-digesting bacteria to break down the fat in sewage before it can mount up to fatberg levels. In many countries, schemes are publicising the issue and urging restaurants and householders not to dump cooking oil, fats and wet wipes into sewers.

WATER WORKS

Thames Water maintains 108,000 km of sewers in and around London. Each year it clears as many as 75,000 blockages, many caused by fatbergs. In 2016, it even released a promotional Christmas song on YouTube called 'Jingle Bells, Sewer Smells'!

⬇ This bus in Sweden runs on biofuel.

WASTE WATCH

Here are some ways to fight fatbergs at home.

- Always scrape leftover food into the food waste caddy or put it outside for birds to eat.

- Use a strainer in the sink to catch food left behind in the washing up water.

- Wipe fat and grease from pans and plates with paper towels before washing-up.

- Let cooking oil cool completely before pouring it into a plastic container with a sealable lid. Many supermarkets and recycling centres have special sections for cooking oil.

FAT INTO FUEL

Schemes in some cities, including Atlanta and San Francisco in the United States, are recycling FOGs into biofuels. These are then used to heat buildings and power school buses. The waste fats, oils and greases are heated and chemicals added to help break them down into useful substances.

13

ISLANDS OF RUBBISH

The 1,200 small coral islands that form the Indian Ocean nation of the Maldives are a popular holiday destination. Tourists seeking unspoilt beaches flock to these islands, but one is anything but a tropical paradise. The entire island of Thilafushi is one giant rubbish dump.

↓ Large mounds of rubbish form Thilafushi's landscape. Some of the rubbish is harmful to life.

PACKED-IN PEOPLE

Thilafushi began life not as an island but a tropical lagoon (a stretch of water enclosed by sandbars and reefs) lying 4 km away from Malé, the capital of the Maldives. Malé is one of the most densely-packed cities in the world, with over 23,000 people living within each built-up square km – over four times the population density of London.

↓ Malé's population has doubled six times since 1987. Now, there is barely any space left.

The Maldives' population of 392,000 is eclipsed by the more than 1.6 million tourists who visit the islands each year. Tourists each generate more than twice the level of waste of the local inhabitants – around 3.5 kg of rubbish per day. It all has to go somewhere, but the Maldives' total land area is a measly 298 km² – only about three-quarters of the size of the Isle of Wight. The solution at the start of the 1990s was to dump waste into holes dug into the lagoon's sand to form a small island.

A GROWING PROBLEM

Since 1992, the dumping has increased to the point that now over 300 tonnes of rubbish is carried by ships (mostly from Malé) to the island every day. Thilafushi has grown and grown. The island is now over 7 km long and occupies an area bigger than the Vatican City. Some of its area has been leased to heavy industries, such as cement works, which cause further waste and pollution.

↑ This vessel is transporting yet more rubbish to Thilafushi.

GOING NOWHERE

Many forms of rubbish take their time to decompose (rot away). A milk carton can take five years, leather items five-to-eight times as long. Plastic bottles may take 450 years and disposable nappies 500-700 years. Glass bottles may take over a million years! It all means that much of the waste and the island itself is unlikely to disappear any time soon, even while other islands in the Maldives are under threat from rising sea levels.

POISONED PARADISE

The waste that arrives at Thilafushi may contain toxic chemicals, such as mercury and lead, or dangerous materials, such as asbestos, some of which pollute the waters around the island. Storms and sea surges can sometimes wash away some of the dumped rubbish. This drifts around the ocean, harms marine life or washes up on the shores of other islands.

OTHER ISLANDS

It's not just in the Maldives. Other small island groups in the Caribbean, Indian Ocean and the Pacific are struggling to deal with their own population's growing rubbish problem. The situation is often made worse by tourist visitors and passenger cruise ships.

REDUCING WASTE

Some of Thilafushi's rubbish is now sorted to recover metals for recycling, or is shipped to India where it is burned to generate energy. Campaign groups such as Zero Waste Maldives are urging businesses to be less wasteful. Hotels and resorts are using less packaging and fewer plastics in favour of materials which can be recycled or composted. Kurumba Resort, for example, has its own recycling centre which composts all food waste and grinds glass down to sand. As a result, it has reduced the amount of rubbish it produces by 70 per cent.

† Rubbish piles up and burns on the side of a road on the Indonesian island of Banda Neira, creating a health hazard. Amateur attempts to burn such piles can lead to dangerous air pollution and the risk of forest fires.

RUINED RIVERS

For thousands of years, rivers have been vital to humans, providing fresh water for them and their crops and livestock and acting as transport links to other communities. They also provided habitats for thousands of different species of fish, marine insects and other living things. But many rivers have been used as dumping grounds for human waste, household rubbish and much more besides, making their waters unfit to drink or live in.

↓ A scientist in protective clothing takes a water sample at the edge of a river poisoned by hazardous waste.

HUMAN HARM

Billions of people around the world do not have the clean water treatment and sewage-removing systems others take for granted. Instead, human waste may enter the very same rivers people drink from, putting them at risk. According to the World Health Organization, more than 360,000 under-fives die each year from diarrhoea caused by unclean water and poor sanitation, much of this related to dirty rivers.

SUPER-POLLUTED RIVER

The Citarum is the longest river in West Java, Indonesia, relied upon by millions of people in the region. It is also one of the world's most polluted rivers. More than 2,000 factories and industrial plants are located along its 270-km length. Many of them use chemicals to dye and treat fabrics and dump waste chemicals including toxic mercury, arsenic and lead into the river. The Citarum contains more than 13 times the safe levels of mercury and almost 1,000 times more lead than is found in safe drinking water.

If that wasn't enough, the river has been used as a watery waste dump by local people. Tonnes of household waste and animal manure enter the water each day. In places, it is impossible to paddle boats through the water due to the mountains of floating rubbish on the surface. In 2018, a seven year clean-up campaign was announced by Indonesia's president but experts think it may take decades for the river to become even remotely clean and healthy.

FARM HARM

The world's farms use 26 times more chemical pesticides and fertilisers than they did 50 years ago, according to the World Wildlife Fund. When rain falls, some of these chemicals (particularly nitrates and phosphates) may be washed off the land as run-off and into streams and rivers. There, they may fuel an explosion of algae growth which causes other river plants to die and the water's oxygen levels to drop sharply. This can kill fish and other aquatic life, depriving other creatures in a food chain of their food and reducing life in and around the river.

↓ **Dead fish float in the polluted waters of the Rio del Plata. The estuary sits between Argentina in the south and Uruguay in the north.**

↑ Sometimes waste water contains toxic chemicals and metals, which can build up in a river and cause harm to living things.

FOUL FACTORIES

Billions of litres of water are used in industry as a coolant, to dilute chemicals and to clean products and machines. Many factories and industries discharge their waste water straight into rivers. In 2013, a Chinese chemicals factory in Hubei province dumped waste ammonia into the nearby Fuhe River. The authorities cleared the river of more than 100,000 kg of fish that had been poisoned and killed by the waste.

CLEANING RIVERS

It takes a lot of work to turn a waste-ruined river around. New laws, if enforced well, can help stop further waste entering a river. Treating sewage to remove harmful bacteria can help stop the spread of disease. Some rivers have oxygen added to them to revitalise them. Volunteers can clean up a river's banks and shallow waters of larger pieces of rubbish. The Thames21 charity, for example, clears over 1,000 tonnes of rubbish from the River Thames in London, UK every year.

→ **This group of volunteers is helping to clear rubbish from a river in the Philippines.**

↓ **'Bubble boats' like this one can help reoxygenate river water.**

BACK FROM THE DEAD

After centuries of sewage and industrial waste polluting the River Thames, in 1957 the Natural History Museum declared the river to be biologically dead. Its waters could no longer support fish and other river-dwelling creatures. A decades-long clean-up followed, helped by better sewage treatment plants and supported by new laws that banned waste-dumping by industry. The river regained high enough levels of oxygen to support a great array of wildlife, which today includes 125 species of fish, 400 species of insects and other invertebrates, as well as many water birds. Even seals and dolphins have been spotted swimming in its waters.

→ **Egyptian geese perch by the Thames. These wild geese feast on river bank plants that only grow when the river isn't heavily polluted.**

GIANT LANDFILLS

Municipal solid waste is the rubbish we are all familiar with – the waste packaging, paper, plastic bottles and other items we throw away each day. It all has to go somewhere. Some of it is burnt in incinerator plants but much enters large pits known as landfills. Landfills occupy huge areas of land and there are lots of them – an estimated half a million in Europe alone!

WEALTHY WORLD WASTE

People in some wealthier nations generate much more municipal solid waste than others. The United States, for example, is home to around four per cent of the world's population but produces 12 per cent of all the world's municipal solid waste. Each man, woman and child in the US generates an average of 773 kg per year. In contrast, a UK inhabitant generates 463 kg and a person in Colombia 232 kg.

STATS OF SHAME

Each person in the USA, on average, generates their own body weight in waste once every six weeks!

BURIED PROBLEMS

Early landfills were just large holes dug in the ground with little thought given to the consequences. As the waste slowly decomposed, water seeping through the rubbish picked up chemicals, traces of metals and poisons. This liquid, called leachate, drained through the ground, contaminating soil and underground water. Rotting rubbish also gives off a lot of waste gases, especially methane, which can explode or catch fire easily. Each year there are over 8,000 landfill fires in the United States alone. Modern landfills are now lined to protect ground and water from leachate.

FRESH KILLS

Between 1955 and 2001, when it closed, Fresh Kills on New York's Staten Island was thought of as the world's largest landfill. It only opened in 1948 as a temporary measure but quickly became the dumping ground for most of New York City's waste.

Amongst the vast quantities of rubbish dumped at Fresh Kills were many tonnes of medical waste. This included thousands of syringes, 90 per cent of which were found to be infected with HIV (human immunodeficiency virus), a virus that attacks the body's immune system and makes it less able to fight off infection.

→ **Fresh Kills covered an area four times larger than the European nation of Monaco.**

DEADLY DUMP

In many parts of the world, desperately poor people scour landfills for rags, bottles or other items they can sell for scrap or recycling to survive. These pickers, some as young as four or five, risk cuts from jagged metal, sharp glass and needles as well as contact with harmful chemicals and poisons.

↑ Child landfill pickers in the Indian city of Delhi may earn less than £1.50 for a day's backbreaking work.

REUSE, REPAIR, RECYCLE

Rubbish that ends up in landfill is not just a waste of what's thrown away but also of the land and energy used to dispose of it. Reusing and repairing old items rather than buying new ones, and recycling objects can reduce much of the waste that heads to landfill.

↓ Searching for items to recycle or sell in a landfill in Surabaya, Indonesia.

LIFE AFTER LANDFILL

Much work is needed to safely complete a landfill site once it's full. The waste mounds need to be capped – sealed from the outside – usually using layers of plastic, clay, rock and earth. A methane collection system of pipes and pumps is also installed to tap the waste gases generated by the rotting rubbish.

With the land unsuitable for building on, some former landfills are being turned into parks or nature reserves, such as Thurrock Thameside Nature Park, east of London. Fresh Kills (see page 23) is also slowly being converted into a giant park, with its first section opened in 2012. By 2037, the park site will cover a vast area of 890 hectares (equivalent to about 1,220 football pitches).

ACTION AT APEX

Today, the USA's biggest active landfill is the Apex landfill, 32 km north of Las Vegas. It receives over 8,500 tonnes of rubbish every day packed into cells lined with plastic. More than 100 m of packed earth and rock lie between the landfill and underground water supplies to stop contamination. Large amounts of methane given off by the rubbish is collected and used to generate electricity for 4,000 homes.

↓ Thurrock Thameside Nature Park has been landscaped with woodlands, meadows and mud flats to attract a wide range of plants and creatures.

THE PROBLEMS WITH PLASTIC

Synthetic plastics are a twentieth-century invention. These plastics, such as polystyrene (invented in 1929), polyvinyl chloride (PVC, 1933) and nylon (1935), were quickly thought of as wonder materials. They proved cheap to produce, hardwearing, light in weight and easy to shape and mould into products. They also proved extremely long-lasting, which has become a massive problem as mountains of plastic waste build up and up.

NOT ROTTING

In our daily lives we're surrounded by plastic, from drinks bottles and toothbrushes to clothing and even some banknotes. Most plastics are made from fossil fuels, such as coal and oil — around six per cent of all oil produced is used in plastics production. Many plastics take five, six or more human lifetimes (450 years or more) to biodegrade and break down. This means that not a single product made of these plastics has yet fully broken down naturally.

→ Plastics production has increased 200 times since 1950. The results of plastic waste now litter beaches and the countryside.

WILDLIFE IN DANGER

Plastics form much of the litter people discard thoughtlessly on land, where it can cause great harm to other living things. Birds, fish and small mammals can get entangled in or strangled by plastic netting, fishing line, cord, bags and the plastic ring carriers used to hold drink cans together. Some creatures – from crabs to frogs and small fish – can get trapped inside larger plastic containers, while plastic bags and films can clog up burrows and small streams. If an animal eats some brightly coloured plastic, thinking of it as food, it lodges in their gut and may kill them.

SINGLE-USE PLASTICS

Around 40 per cent of the 400 million tonnes of plastic produced globally each year is used for single-use objects, such as drinking straws, bags and coffee cups (many of which are made of paper but with a waterproof plastic lining). These objects are used once, sometimes for seconds, before they are binned. The use of these items can be easily avoided, by using a refillable bottle or cup for drinks and carrying a reusable bag for shopping.

27

TACKLING PLASTIC

Successful campaigning to highlight the problems with plastic is now resulting in governments and businesses taking action, particularly on single-use plastics. In 2018, for example, Seattle became the first US city to ban plastic drinking straws and cutlery. The first nation to ban lightweight, single-use plastic bags was Bangladesh back in 2002. It was only in 2015 that the UK took action, placing a 5p tax (rising to 10p in 2020) on each single-use plastic bag. Sales of such bags have since dropped by more than four-fifths.

↑ Shoppers around the world are encouraged to choose reusable bags over single-use plastic bags.

→ A heart-shaped recycling container in Bulgaria is filled with plastic bottle caps for the 'Caps for the Future' charity in Bulgaria. The charity recycles the bottle caps and buys baby incubators for local hospitals with the proceeds.

RECYCLING PLASTICS

Those plastics that can be recycled have many potential uses. PET plastic, used to make many drinks bottles, for instance, is often recycled into fabric for fleeces and filling for cushions. Recycling not only stops plastic waste, it can also save the energy and raw materials that would otherwise be used to make new plastic products. Recycling just one plastic drinks bottle, for example, can save enough energy to power a 60 watt light bulb for up to six hours.

→ In Germany, placing a plastic bottle into this automatic machine gives you a credit voucher in return.

BOTTLE SCHEMES

Consumers in 40 countries around the world, receive a small refund when they return recyclable plastic bottles. The aim is to encourage higher rates of recycling. In Germany and Norway, for example, this has resulted in 95 per cent of all plastic drinks bottles being recycled.

← Building a house out of plastic bottles filled with sand in the city of Kaduna, Nigeria. Nigerians throw away three million plastic bottles each day. Similar homes and buildings have been built in Algeria, Panama and El Salvador.

REUSING PLASTICS

Plastics can be reused in innovative ways at home. Plastic bottles can be turned into plant holders or storage jars and even, when filled with sand or earth, used as a home-building material. In Haiti, where people drink fresh water out of plastic pouches, the Peace Cycle organisation sews together thousands of these empty pouches to make sturdy shopping bags to sell to customers around the world. This cuts back on waste and reduces reliance on single-use plastic.

STATS OF SHAME

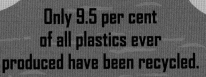

Only 9.5 per cent of all plastics ever produced have been recycled.

29

ALL AT SEA

Water can carry lightweight plastics long distances from where they were originally thrown away. Billions of pieces of plastic litter are swept along rivers, streams and down sewer pipes into the world's oceans. There, this waste mixes with plastic containers, fishing lines and nets and other plastic waste dumped overboard by ships. The total is a frightening amount – an estimated eight million tonnes of plastic waste (around 790 Eiffel Towers' worth) is dumped into the world's oceans each year.

↓ Barnacles and other marine creatures have latched onto this plastic bottle in the Pacific Ocean.

STATS OF SHAME

Eating plastic kills an estimated one million sea birds and 100,000 marine animals each year, according to the United Nations.

WASHED-UP WASTE

It only takes a tiny fraction of the waste plastic in the ocean to wash up and swamp shorelines and islands. In 2015, researchers discovered that the remote Henderson Island in the Pacific Ocean had been overwhelmed by plastic. They found an average of 671 pieces of plastic waste littering each square metre of the island's beaches.

↑ Plastics can destroy shore habitats and harm the creatures who live and feed there.

THE MENACE OF MICROPLASTICS

Many plastics break down into microscopic pieces known as microplastics. Other sources are artificial fabrics, such as acrylic or polyester, which shed tiny microplastic fibres when they're washed, and microbeads – tiny particles added to some toothpastes and cosmetics as an abrasive. Both are fine enough to pass through filters and sewage treatments and enter the ocean in large quantities.

Trillions of microplastics are found in the world's oceans. They can turn water cloudy and prevent marine plants accessing enough sunlight to grow. The harmful chemicals they contain, such as polychlorinated biphenyls (PCBs), can enter the bodies of feeding marine creatures. These travel up a food chain as the creatures are eaten. According to the Marine Conservation Society, a typical European person who eats seafood also consumes 11,000 microplastic particles each year.

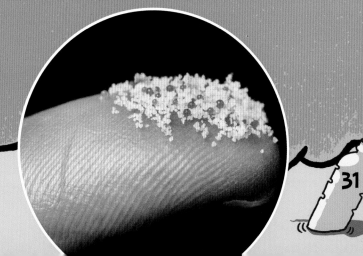

→ A single 200 ml tube of some facial scrubs can contain over three million plastic beads.

Much of the plastic that floats in the world's oceans becomes concentrated in certain areas due to circular ocean currents called gyres. These are caused by the Earth's rotation and the planet's winds. As the current rotates, solid particles of rubbish, mostly plastic, gradually drift towards the centre of the gyre. There are five major gyres in the world's oceans – one in the Indian Ocean and two in each of the Atlantic and Pacific oceans.

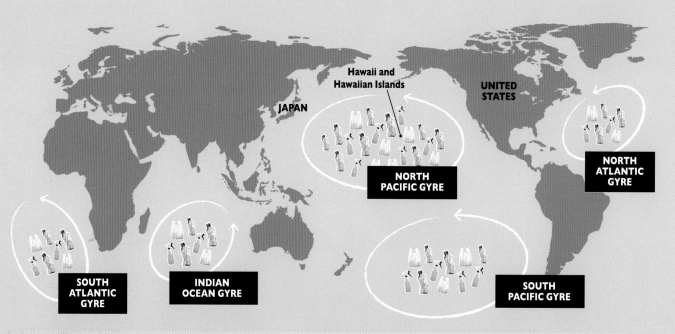

Hawaii and Hawaiian Islands

JAPAN

UNITED STATES

NORTH PACIFIC GYRE

NORTH ATLANTIC GYRE

SOUTH ATLANTIC GYRE

INDIAN OCEAN GYRE

SOUTH PACIFIC GYRE

THE GREAT PACIFIC GARBAGE PATCH

The gyre in the north Pacific is home to a gigantic accumulation of plastic waste known as the Great Pacific Garbage Patch. It's actually two large patches in one – the eastern part exists between the Hawaiian Islands and the west coast of the United States, while the western patch is found between Hawaii and Japan.

The two patches range over a wide area (as large as 1.6 million km or three times the size of France) and are estimated to contain 1.8 trillion pieces of plastic.

↓ **The Great Garbage Patch consists of larger pieces of plastic waste, such as fishing nets and bottles, as well as a cloudy soup of broken-down microplastics.**

A group of students help clean up plastic waste from Mumbai's Chowpatty beach in India.

SEIZING BACK THE SEAS

Campaigns highlighting the perils of plastics seek to increase awareness and decrease the use and waste of plastics. A number of nations have banned microbeads, including France and the UK in 2018 and Italy and India in 2020. Increasing numbers of clean-up campaigns have taken place on shores and in shallow waters to remove plastic waste that could wash back out to sea.

THE OCEAN CLEANUP

At the age of 18, Dutch teenager Boyan Slat founded The Ocean Cleanup organisation and invented an ingenious C-shaped boom system. It floated in the ocean and collected plastic waste on or just below the water's surface. Following successful trials, it is hoped that a number of these booms could remove half of the Great Pacific Garbage Patch in just five years.

In a June 2019 trial, the Ocean Cleanup system collected over 40,000 kg of plastic waste.

WHAT A DUMP!

Some dumps are designed to accept just one type or category of waste. Whenever someone throws away an electronic item – from a hairdryer or toaster to an old phone or laptop – they are generating e-waste. With rapid changes in technology, more and more electrical objects have been thrown away in favour of bright, new shiny upgrades, creating an increasingly large e-waste problem. Around 50 million tonnes of e-waste is produced each year – about the weight of 151 Empire State Buildings or 4,950 Eiffel Towers!

E-WASTE

Electronic goods are made of many different materials, making them hard to recycle easily, According to the United Nations, only one fifth of the all e-waste is tracked and recycled properly. Much of the remainder ends up in landfill and dumps. There, toxic substances found in the waste's circuit boards and components often seep into and contaminate soil, streams and rivers. In China's Guiyu area, where many people specialise in taking circuit boards apart to recover metals, extremely high levels of poisonous metals, such as lead, cadmium and mercury, were discovered in the soil and local water supplies.

34

AGBOGBLOSHIE

On the outskirts of Ghana's biggest city, Accra, lies what is thought of as being the world's biggest e-waste dump. The Agbogbloshie district (left) contains hundreds of wooden shack workshops and sheds around the dump where many people, mostly teens and young men, scavenge broken electronic goods for the tiny amounts of silver and other valuable metals they contain.

BURNING ISSUE

At Agbogbloshie, highly sought-after copper is recovered by burning electrical wiring to remove its plastic insulation. This creates harmful air pollution, leading to nausea and breathing problems. Waste pickers clamber through the mountains of rubbish. They risk cuts and infection from dirty glass, sharp plastic and metal and contact with poisonous substances.

➡ **Two young men at Agbogbloshie burn electrical cabling, inhaling some of the toxic fumes found in the billowing smoke.**

WASTE ON WHEELS

More than 1.1 billion motor vehicles are found on the world's roads. The tyres they run on tend to wear out after travelling an average of 30,000 km. The vehicle owner replaces the tyres without much thought to what happens to the discarded rubber. In the past, these tyres were mostly thrown away at large dumps or buried at landfill sites.

TYRE CEMETERY

The largest-known purpose-built tyre landfill is found in the Middle Eastern nation of Kuwait. The Sulaibiya 'tyre cemetery' houses as many as 14 million tyres, some from its own country but also imported for disposal from India, Malaysia and elsewhere. These tyres are all placed in giant holes dug in the desert. The tyre dump has sprawled to cover an area of around 600,000 square metres – almost the size of the entire Disneyland theme park in California in the US. Water which collects in the tyre holes can stagnate and provide an ideal breeding ground for malaria-carrying mosquitoes.

TYRES ON FIRE

Rubber burns and acts as a potent fuel if a collection of waste tyres catches fire. Such fires can be extremely difficult to put out. A 1998 fire at a tyre waste disposal centre in California took 26 months to extinguish!

A fire broke out at Sulaibiya's tyre dumps in April 2012, and it took hundreds of firefighters to bring it under control. As tyres burn, they can release toxic substances, including carbon monoxide, arsenic, benzene and sulphur oxides into the atmosphere, causing severe air pollution.

NEW USES FOR OLD TYRES

Many US states and, since 2006, the European Union have banned the disposal of tyres in landfills and dumps. Instead, waste tyres have to be processed or recycled in some way. Many tyres are burned in giant kilns to produce heat for cement-making industries. Some tyres are re-moulded and given a brand new tread for grip before being sold as retread tyres. Others are recycled or repurposed in ingenious ways – as sea barriers to prevent coastal erosion, for example, or as seating, flower beds or children's toys (right).

CRUMBS!

Millions of tyres are pulped and processed into a rubber crumb. This raw material can then be moulded, dyed and turned into a variety of other products, including surfaces for children's playgrounds, sports pitches and rubber tracks. Some crumb is used for rubber matting and underlay – the rubbery layer below the top surface of carpet.

37

SPACE WASTE

Not only have we humans littered our own planet with vast amounts of waste of many different kinds, we've also gone further and created some waste that is out of this world.

LUNAR JUNKYARD

Just twelve men, all astronauts on NASA's Apollo missions between 1969 and 1972, have stood on the Moon, but they left quite a junkyard behind on the lunar surface. Not only were completed experiments and the descent module sections of their spacecraft left behind to save weight, so were hundreds of other items. The list includes empty food packages, various tools, three lunar rover vehicles, 12 pairs of boots, backpacks, used wet wipes, blankets and 96 bags of human wee, poo and vomit!

← A pile of rubbish is clearly visible to the left of several science experiments which were conducted on the Moon by the crew of Apollo 17 in 1972.

ORBITING DEBRIS

↓ This NASA image depicts the debris orbiting Earth within 2,000 km of the planet's surface.

Surrounding Earth is a surprisingly large amount of junk created by human endeavour. Parts of spacecraft that were jettisoned during their mission, old rocket stages and satellites, lost tools and pieces of machines which have exploded or been destroyed in space, all orbit Earth.

According to the European Space Agency, in 2019 there were 34,000 known items of space debris 10 cm or larger travelling around Earth. A further 900,000 1-10 cm pieces existed, as well as millions of sub-centimetre sized fragments. Even small pieces, such as a single bolt or fleck of paint, racing around Earth at speeds of up to 28,000 km/h could cause severe damage on impact.

SATELLITE CRASH

Space is so vast that collisions are rare, but when they occur, they can be catastrophic. In 1996, a French military satellite called Cerise was destroyed by fragments from a French rocket that had broken up ten years earlier. In 2009, Russian satellite Cosmos 2251, that was no longer working, crashed into an active American communications satellite, Iridium 33, destroying it. The collision added more than 2,000 pieces of space debris to those already orbiting Earth.

PROJECT WEST FORD

Between 1961 and 1963, the United States launched 480 million 1.78-cm-long copper needles into orbit 3,500-3,800 km above Earth. These orbiting slivers of copper were designed to create a surface off which radio signals could be bounced. The project was shelved but the needles remain as space junk surrounding Earth.

LOST PROPERTY

Most space junk is made up of parts of old satellites, rockets and spacecraft, but there are some more unusual items too. These include a glove from the first ever US spacewalk in 1965, lost by astronaut Ed White, a spatula dropped by Shuttle astronaut Piers Sellers in 2006 and two years later, an incredibly expensive bag of tools. Heidemarie Stefanyshyn-Piper (pictured right) lost her grip on the bag while on a spacewalk outside the International Space Station in 2008. The tool bag was worth US$100,000 (£80,000) and was tracked for eight months in space.

← In 2003 the space shuttle Columbia exploded in mid-air on its return to Earth. Displayed here are some of the more than 80,000 fragments of the shuttle that showered parts of Texas, Arkansas and Louisiana.

DOWN TO EARTH

Many pieces of space waste are in a low enough orbit that the pull of Earth's gravity eventually draws them back to our planet. This is known as orbital decay. Most, like the glove and tool bag mentioned above, burn up in Earth's atmosphere, but some do make it back to the planet's surface. Only a small handful of people have been slightly injured by glancing blows from small pieces of crashing debris. In 1979, parts of the Skylab space station scattered over the Indian Ocean and parts of Western Australia. A small town in Australia called Esperance sent NASA a AUS$400 (£200) fine for littering!

TRACKING

A system of telescopes and low-light TV cameras catalogue all the space junk orbiting Earth. This GEODSS system (GEODSS is short for Ground-based, Electro-Optical Deep Space Surveillance) also tracks the orbital path of any object above 5 cm in size, so the risk of impact with an active satellite or spacecraft can be calculated.

↑ Found in Haleakalā Crater in a dormant volcano on the Hawaiian Island of Maui, this is one of three GEODSS sites. The other two are located in New Mexico and on the small Indian Ocean island of Diego Garcia.

SOLUTIONS IN SPACE

A number of space agencies are researching ingenious new ways to tackle the problem of space waste. Japan's space agency, JAXA, is designing an electrodynamic tether (EDT), a 700-m-long space whip with a 20 kg weight on the end. This would be unreeled to knock a piece of space junk out of its current orbit so that it would head towards Earth and burn up in the atmosphere. Other machines, such as CleanSpace-1 from Switzerland (above right), throw a net over a broken satellite and then fire rockets to drag themselves and the satellite to destruction in Earth's atmosphere.

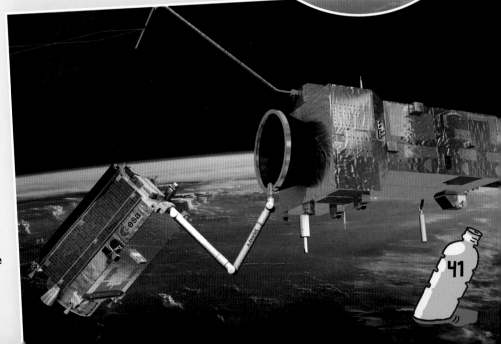

→ The European Space Agency plans to send robots into space to clear away space junk.

YOU v. WASTE

Waste is a massive global problem, but many charities, organisations and councils are making improvements. We can each make a difference, too, by recycling more and reducing the waste we and our families and friends generate in a great variety of ways.

↓ This colourful dolphin mural is made from plastic bottle tops.

42

WASTE NOT WANT NOT

Think before you bin an unwanted item. Could someone else make use of it or could it be repurposed into something else of use? Jeans or tracksuit bottoms can be turned into shorts. T-shirts can be made into cushions, duvet covers or bags. Why not organise a swap shop at school or with friends where you can exchange unwanted clothing, books and media. If you do have shoes, spectacles, books or computing tech that no one wants, look into donating to organisations that will put them to good use.

→ **Two volunteers check and grade unwanted trainers which are then sold in charity shops to raise money or donated to those in need of footwear rather than being thrown away.**

CUT BACK ON DISPOSABLES

Think about how you use plastics and other disposables. Carry a canvas or other non-plastic bag instead of single-use bags, use a refillable water bottle rather than a disposable water bottle, and use washable cloths rather than disposable tissues and wet wipes. Try to buy goods with as little wasteful packaging as possible.

SUCCESS STORY: BYE BYE PLASTIC BAGS

In 2013, Melati and Isabel Wijsen weren't yet in their teens when they founded Bye Bye Plastic Bags. They campaigned hard to remove waste bags on their home island of Bali in Indonesia, fundraising to provide non-plastic alternatives. In the summer of 2019, Bali banned all single-use plastics including bags.

43

CLEAN UP YOUR COMMUNITY

Set yourself and your family, a group of friends or your class the challenge of picking up 10 pieces of rubbish each day or 100 pieces every week. Get your teacher or after-school group leader to organise recycling projects or a clean-up of a local stream, pond or land area you can all take part in. You could have a competition to create fun litter and recycling bins around school, turning them into animals, robots or cartoon characters to encourage others to use them more.

↓ A group of children and adults take part in a clean-up campaign in Bali, Indonesia. Working with others from your community, it is possible to transform waste-ridden environments.

FOOD WASTE

On average, each person in Europe and North America wastes a staggering 95-115 kg of food every year. Cut back on this terrible waste by freezing or using spare food before it goes off. Then get creative and put together a leftovers meal. If you have a garden, get your family into composting! Fill a large container or compost bin with waste fruit and veg, stale bread and cereal, torn up newspaper and grass cuttings. If you add a layer of soil in your bin first, the bacteria and worms in the soil will help speed up the composting process.

↑ After a few months you'll have enough compost to enrich your garden soil naturally without using chemical fertilisers.

WHY BUY?

Before you buy something new, stop and think ... do I really need that? Could I borrow or adapt something I or someone else in my family already has? Your broken bike, ripped jeans or slow-running computer tablet may just need a few tweaks or repairs to transform it.

SUCCESS STORY: ECO-BANK

In 2012, a young Peruvian boy, José Adolfo Quisocala Condori, set up the Bartselana Student Bank for children in his local town. To open an account, kids had to collect at least 5 kg of waste paper or plastic and then deposit at least 1 kg more waste every month. In return, they received a payment into their account, funded by the waste being sold to recycling companies. Jose's eco-bank now has over 2,000 members recycling many tonnes of rubbish throughout Peru.

45

GLOSSARY

atmosphere The blanket of gases that surround the Earth's surface, warming it by trapping heat, filtering out harmful rays from space and providing oxygen for creatures to breathe.

biodegradable Describes a material or substance that breaks down naturally over time. Some items biodegrade in months. Others can take centuries.

compound A substance which is made up of two or more different chemical elements.

contaminate To make something no longer pure by adding a polluting substance or substances.

decompose To rot or break down.

feral Describe wild animals not owned or controlled by people.

incinerator A device used to burn solid waste to dispose of it.

jettison To remove and abandon a part of a spacecraft such as a rocket stage.

landfill A place where waste is disposed of by being buried.

leachate Liquid made of water that has seeped or drained through solid materials carrying a little of the material dissolved within it.

methane A colourless gas which can burn and is the main ingredient of natural gas. Increasing levels of methane in the atmosphere are partly responsible for global warming.

microplastics Very small pieces of plastic (typically under 5 mm in size) that pollute the environment.

municipal solid waste The bags, bottles, cans and other everyday items of waste people in towns and cities throw away each day.

pollution The process by which a substance or material harms an environment in some way.

satellite An object which travels around a planet. Satellites can be natural like the Moon or artificial like weather or environmental satellites which monitor conditions on Earth.

FURTHER INFORMATION

BOOKS

Stand Against: Pollution and Waste
– Georgia Amson-Bradshaw, Franklin Watts, 2020

This Book Is Not Rubbish
– Isabel Thomas, Wren & Rook, 2018

Go Green
– Liz Gogerly, Franklin Watts, 2018

Ecographics: Pollution
– Izzi Howell, Franklin Watts, 2019

Environment Detective Investigates: Making Air Cleaner
– Jen Green, Wayland, 2015

Eco Steam: The Food We Eat
– Georgia Amson-Bradshaw, Wayland, 2018

What A Waste: Rubbish, Recycling, and Protecting our Planet – Jess French, DK, 2019

Guardians of the Planet
– Clive Gifford, Buster Books, 2019

Eco Stories for Those Who Dare to Care –
Ben Hubbard, Franklin Watts, 2020

WEBSITES

ypte.org.uk
Lots of factsheets and ideas for waste-tackling activities can be found on this website produced by the Young People's Trust For The Environment.

kidsagainstplastic.co.uk
The Kids Against Plastic website is packed full of activities and facts about how you can help tackle plastic waste in your area.

science.howstuffworks.com/environmental/green-science/landfill3.htm
How landfills work and how modern landfills are carefully designed.

endplasticwaste.org
The official website of the Alliance To End Plastic Waste is packed full of stats and stories about the issue and ways it can be tackled.

theoceancleanup.com
This website details the extraordinary campaign and machines hoping to rid the oceans of up to 90 per cent of their plastic waste.

education.abc.net.au/home#!/topic/495996/recycling
Learn more about waste impact and recycling at this fun Australian website which contains games and videos.

youtube.com/watch?v=0EyaTqezSzs
An animated video describing research into the Great Pacific Garbage Patch.

recyclenow.com/what-to-do-with
Advice on how to recycle a variety of different objects and materials.

stuffin.space
An extraordinary interactive site where you can explore all the old satellites, rockets and other space junk travelling around Earth and see their orbits.

earthday.org/take-action-now
Information on many campaigns and projects you can do to help tackle waste and pollution.

brightside.me/inspiration-tips-and-tricks/17-ingenious-ideas-to-reuse-plastic-bottles-367160
Seventeen clever ideas to reuse plastic bottles in innovative ways.

INDEX

Agbogbloshie 35
ammonia 20
Apex landfill 25
archaeologists 4
Argentina 20
asbestos 17
astronauts 38, 40
Atlantic Ocean 32
Australia 11, 40

bacteria 13, 21, 45
Bali 43, 44
Bangladesh 28
biodegrade 26
biofuel 13
Bulgaria 28
Bye Bye Plastic Bags 43

carbon monoxide 6, 37
Caribbean 17
cesspits 10
China 20, 34
city 6, 7, 8, 9, 11, 12, 24, 28, 29, 35
clean-up 9, 33, 41, 44
Colombia 22
compost 17, 45
copper 35, 39
cruise ships 17

decompose 16, 23
disease 8, 10, 12, 21
dumps 5, 13, 14, 15, 18, 19, 20, 21, 23, 24, 34, 35, 36, 37

Eco-Bank 45
energy 5, 17, 24, 28
European Space Agency (ESA) 39, 41
e-waste 34, 35

farming 5, 20
fatbergs 10–13
fertilisers 20, 45
flooding 12

flushers 12
fog 7, 8
FOG (fat, oil and grease) 10, 13
food waste 4, 5, 17, 45
fossil fuels 6, 26
Fresh Kills 23, 25

GEODSS 41
Germany 13, 29
Ghana 35
Great Pacific Garbage Patch, the 32, 33
Great Smog, the 8, 9
gyres 32

habitats 5, 18, 31
Haiti 29
Hawaii 32, 41

incinerators 22
India 17, 24, 33, 36
Indian Ocean 14, 17, 32, 40, 41
Indonesia 17, 19, 43
industry 6, 7, 16, 20, 21, 37

Japan 32, 41
JAXA 41

Kids Against Plastic 42
Kuwait 36

landfill 22–25, 34, 36, 37
leachate 23
lead (metal) 17, 19, 34
Lipobak 13
Liverpool 11
London 8, 9, 10, 11, 13, 15, 25

Maldives 14, 15, 16, 17
Malé 15, 16
marine animals 30, 31
mercury 17, 19, 34
methane 23, 25

Mexico City 9
microplastics 31, 32
Monaco 23
'Monster of Whitechapel' 11
Moon 38
municipal solid waste 22

NASA 38, 39, 40
New York City 23
Nigeria 29
nitrogen oxide 7

ocean (see also Atlantic Ocean; Indian Ocean; Pacific Ocean) 17, 30, 31, 32, 33
Ocean Cleanup 33
oxygen 20, 21
ozone 7

Pacific Ocean 17, 30, 31, 32
particulates 7
'pea-soupers' 8
Peru 45
pesticides 20
Philippines 21
pickers 24, 35
pigeons 9
plastic 10, 13, 16, 17, 22, 25, 26–29, 30, 31, 32, 33, 35, 42, 43, 45
poison 17, 18, 20, 23, 24, 34, 35
pollution 5, 16
pollution, air 6–9, 17, 35, 37
pollution, water 18–21
public transport 9

recycling 13, 17, 24, 28, 29, 34, 37, 42, 44, 45
resources 5
reuse 24, 27, 29
Rio de la Plata 20

rivers 10, 18–21, 30, 34
Citarum 19
Fuhe 20
Thames 13, 21
rockets 39, 40, 41
rot 10, 16, 23, 25, 26
rubber 36, 37
rubber crumb 37
run-off 20

sanitation 18
satellites 39, 40, 41
sewage 11, 12, 13, 18, 21, 31
sewers 10, 11, 12, 13, 30
single-use 27, 28, 29, 42, 43
smog 6–9
space junk 38–41
space shuttle 40
Spain 11
Sulaibiya 36, 37
sulphur dioxide 6
Sweden 13

Thailand 7
Thilafushi 14–17
Thurrock Thameside Nature Park 25
tourists 14, 15, 17
toxic 7, 17, 19, 20, 34, 35, 37
tyres 36–37

UK 10, 11, 12, 22, 28, 33
United Nations 5, 30, 34
USA 4, 13, 22, 23, 25, 28, 32, 36, 37, 39, 40

València 11
volatile organic compounds (VOCs) 7

wildlife 5, 21, 27
World Health Organization 7, 18